PRAYER WARRIOR

INTERCESSORY PRAYER
TAKING IT TO ANOTHER NEXT LEVEL

God will teach us as we seek Him

I am by no means an expert on intercessory prayer, though I have functioned in it for many years now. Having served as a missionary, a pastor, a worship leader, and a mother, it is to our advantage to learn the most effective ways of intercessory prayer. So here in this book I will share what I have learned over many years and what has brought the most results. I will share revelations that the Lord has shared with me. I believe we are to be continually learning. One will never know ALL there is, but God will teach us as we seek Him. The Holy Spirit is the best teacher one can have. So, lets get started, there is so much goodness that God has in store!

Taking it to the sky

Let's start by looking at the eagle. Did you know the eagle does not fight the snake on the ground? The eagle will pick it up and take the snake up into the sky. This changes the battle ground. The snake has no stamina, no power, and no balance in the air. It is useless, weak, and vulnerable in the sky. On the ground the snake is powerful wise and deadly. The eagle has taken the serpent to a place where he holds the upper hand.

I have read that the eagle is the only natural predator the snake has. Some animals can kill a snake, but the eagle not only will kill it, but he also hunts it for food! That alone should excite the warrior within you! We are going to look into taking our enemy into the heavens. We will look at arming our prayers with Kingdom weapons.

The power of His name

You can take your fight into the spirit realm by engaging heaven. This is something that is available to every Christian. So how do I get there? First you must have Jesus setting on the throne in your heart. When you receive Christ as Lord you are able to use the power, He has given to us to overcome. *Mark 16:17-18 says, "And these signs shall follow them* *that believe; <u>In my name</u> shall they cast out devils; they shall speak with new tongues; 18They shall take up serpents; and if they drink any deadly thing, it shall not hurt them; they shall lay hands on the sick, and they shall recover."* Jesus has handed the power of His name to you. He has our back! *Luke 10:19 "Behold, I give unto you power to tread on serpents and scorpions, and over all the power of the enemy: and nothing shall by any means hurt you."*

... For I will contend with him who contends with you." (Isaiah 49:25)

How to fight a supernatural battle

Let's look at how to fight a supernatural battle. When we learn the art of war we will take the enemy out of his territory, out of his comfort zone and we will battle in the spirit realm. It is in this realm that you can fight as a kingdom warrior, one who fights in the supernatural. It isn't our physical being that can fight a spiritual war only our spirit.

Learning to wield the weapons of our warfare which are not carnal but mighty through God will give you an advantage. *"For the weapons of our warfare are not carnal, but mighty through God to the pulling down of strong holds;" 2 Corinthians 10:4.*

In *Ephesians 6:10-18* KJV we find a list of our armor and a definition of each piece. A wise intercessor will clothe themselves in God's amor. Let's read the list again. *10 "Finally, my brethren, be strong in the Lord, and in the power of his might.11 Put on the whole armor of God, that ye may be able to stand against the wiles of the devil.*

12 For we wrestle not against flesh and blood, but against principalities, against powers, against the rulers of the darkness of this world, against spiritual wickedness in high places. 13 Wherefore take unto you the whole armor of God, that ye may be able to withstand in the evil day, and having done all, to stand. 14 Stand therefore, having your loins girt about with truth, and having on the breastplate of righteousness; 15 And your feet shod with the preparation of the gospel of peace; 16 Above all, taking the shield of faith, wherewith ye shall be able to quench all the fiery darts of the wicked. 17 And take the helmet of salvation, and the sword of the Spirit, which is the word of God: 18 Praying always with all prayer and supplication in the Spirit and watching thereunto with all perseverance and supplication for all saints.

Let's look at the word "carnal". It is sarkikós - pertaining to flesh, i.e. (by extension) bodily, temporal, or (by implication) animal, unregenerate:--carnal, fleshly.

Our weapons are not "carnal", so they are not fleshly. We tend to lose battles when we bring our warfare into the carnal realm, and we let our physical emotions take sides.

When we fight in the heavenlies we will view the enemy with heaven's vision of the battle, not an earthly vision of the battle. It is like when you see your street through your eyes right now, you see four or five houses, but when you are in an airplane over your neighborhood you can see many houses and for many miles. The view changes from what is right before you to a view of the beginning, the middle, and even the end.

As an intercessor functioning at a higher level, you can see heaven's view of the battle. You don't fret over what you see because thru the eyes of faith you can see the result. There is a peace that this intercessor has in their life because they already see the victory.

I know several prayer warriors, that I would call on in a time of need and I know beyond a doubt that they would shake heaven with their war cry. Those are the ones you want praying on your behalf. I can literally picture them in my mind grabbing up the serpent, soaring into the spirit realm and then pulling the serpent's head off as victory is won!

Don't get me wrong it is still very much war, but with our spiritual armor on we won't just fight, we win!

Prayers are always good but sometimes you need to know that you have touched heaven. You want results for what you are praying about. Praying into the will of the Father is another way to see fast results. In that case there isn't time spend arguing or demanding your way from the Father but you are already in agreement with Him. Learning to feel and sense the Father's heart is very important. When you feel that you know where the spirit is leading pray into it.

The Keeper of the Book

A vision

As I lay before the Lord in prayer, I saw myself standing in a room adjacent to the court rooms in heaven. It seemed I was standing at the corner of a huge table. As my eyes looked up the leg of the table and my eyes neared the top of the table, I saw a large sleeve on an arm that was writing in a book. I seemed to be small compared to the table and the arm that I was seeing.

As I prayed for this one, and that one when the words would leave my mouth the one writing would pull a page out of the book and it would fall to the floor. I was wondering what the pages had on them that were being pulled out of the book and dropped to the floor as if they were trash and not needed anymore. I noticed that if I was praying against a sickness or any issue, the page that the illness had been written on was pulled from the book of that person's life. It was totally removed! If I prayed for anything to be healed, removed, or transformed, it was pulled from that person's book and it was not there anymore. Thru payer the life was changed! Our prayers changed the outcome, so the pages were removed and thrown on the floor!

Prayer is a necessity. It is vastly important! We can change things when we cry out to God!

The keeper of the books will edit the pages when we pray for a change!

If we say and do-nothing things will continue down the path. Bring a change! Bring a healing! Bring a changed heart! Bring a changed destination! Speak it out to the Lord!

Second-Tier Intercessor

A few months back Rusty & I had COVID. We were both so sick and one night his temperature got up to 103.9. I was trying to cool his head with a cold cloth. Later in the night he had gotten up and made it to the bathroom. As I was in and out of sleep I was startled as he yelled "God! Save me!" I could hear him moaning. I was frightened because he was so sick. Later he was able to tell me that he had cried out to God for help as he saw a black goo coming down over him. He said it looked like the black symbiotic goo that came down over Venom in the Marvel movie. It was there to suffocate the life out of him. He said that as he called out to the Lord, the Lord spoke to him and said, "You have two second tier intercessors praying for you". That was a term we hadn't heard of before. He said the Lord showed him the face of one of them. We began to inquire what was a second-tier intercessor? What did God mean? After praying about this term, the Lord used, and doing some studying, a second tier-intercessor is one who functions from a heavenly perspective instead of an earthly one. He is not motivated out of his or her emotions but is only moved by heaven in prayer. Most of our prayer life is reactionary to the events going on around us, but a second-tier intercessor will become proactive as he or she is moved by heaven. It's like the eagle who takes the snake out of his environment and fights him in the sky. This gives the eagle a great advantage over the enemy. Understanding how to function by faith, from the heavens, will make it easier to win our battles and easier to obtain victory.

It was comforting to know about the two intercessors and that God was already on the case!

I have and do function in the courts of heaven. You can take an issue to the courts of heaven. In the court room you will state the issue and why it is unjust, and you may ask for it to be resolved. You want to only enter the courts of heaven with a pure heart. The courts there function very similar to the courts here on earth. I have seen justice given on behalf of someone close to me. Just like Haman's gallows', (Esther 7:9) we witnessed the tables turn on a party who was wrongly accusing someone. God handed out justice and in that case the person bringing the injustice had everything done to them that they were trying to do to the party we represented in the courts. God is a just God.

Now God had called an audible about the second-tier intercessor and this makes one back up and look at how effective is our intercessory prayer.

Let's kick it up a notch. Let's come into agreement with heaven. Let's ask the Father to train us in this. He will show us and teach us if we just ask. Don't assume you already have it all because there is always room to learn and room to grow.

As we come into agreement with heaven, let's unite in faith believing that nothing is impossible with God. Nothing has ever stopped Him! When we operate as a second-tier intercessor warring from the heavens we will stand with power and peace, knowing God will fight for us!

"The Lord will fight for you, and you shall hold your peace." (Exodus 14:14)

"Crazy Prays"

"And ye shall seek me, and find me, when ye shall search for me with all your heart." Jer. 29:13

Searching for God with a whole heart. Those pesky adjectives and adverbs just keep popping up when you read the scriptures. The "whole heart" is a theme that you will find throughout all the Bible. I assume it means a "whole" heart as opposed to "half" a heart. It implies "undivided" attention. The adverb or adjective used to define your spiritual life would determine how your defined in heaven. 😕 "Half baked", "lukewarm", hhhmm, how are you defined? I was describing a sister in the church the other day and I said she "crazy prays"; meaning she prays like crazy. Yes, "crazy prays", is what I meant. 🙂 If you're not getting results or experiencing the kingdom, maybe, just maybe you ought to learn the principle of "crazy prays." She has been having some over the top experiences in Heaven and yes, it is because she "prays like crazy!' You can experience the Kingdom too when you learn to "pray like crazy".

"Seek Him with your whole heart"

You may also be interested in my other books on prayer and spiritual warfare. They are available on Amazon.com and other places books are sold.

Supernatural Adventures in Prayer

Kingdom Shield Maiden

Communing with the Father

Ministering with the Angels

www.ingramcontent.com/pod-product-compliance
Lightning Source LLC
Chambersburg PA
CBHW021331160726
47994CB00004B/1712